This Book belongs to *Rachel Coulan*

**Leeson Park School of Music**

D1671224

TO MY YOUNGEST SON

SINGING RASCALS Pentatonic
Original Finnish title LAULUVIIKARI

This series of books is based on the teaching method developed by
Géza Szilvay and is part of the instructional material
used by the Colourstrings Music Kindergartens.

The melodies in the SINGING RASCALS series reappear in the colourstrings/
colourkeys instrumental beginners books. Pupils find this
very helpful during the early stages of learning an instrument.

For further details of
Colourstrings Music Kindergartens
write to the publishers:

COLOURSTRINGS INTERNATIONAL LIMITED
4 ULLSWATER CLOSE
KINGSTON VALE
LONDON SW15 3RF

Printed by Breckland Print Ltd, Attleborough, Norfolk, England

ISBN 1 873604 01 7

# SINGING RASCALS

PENTATONIC

Géza Szilvay

Illustrations:
**Tuulia Hyrske**

Words:
**Angela Ailes**

SONGS:

COLOURSTRINGS INTERNATIONAL LIMITED
LONDON

# LOOK LAMB LOOK

*SO*    *MI*

Look Lamb look.    See my pret-ty kite fly,

with the swal-lows so high. Look lamb look.

SO

MI

# HARRY HARE

Har-ry Hare is in a hur-ry, full of care and full of wor-ry.

Har-ry Hare is late for tea. What a naugh-ty hare is he!

LA

SO

MI

# HEY BEETLE !

SO MI DO

"Hey bee-tle, say bee-tle, is your lar-der bare? My worm you can share."

"Thank you but I'm far too shy," said the bee-tle pas-sing by.

6

SO

MI

DO

# SQUIRREL

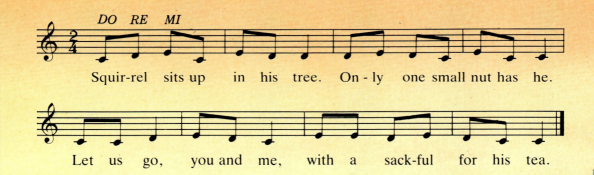

*DO  RE  MI*

Squir-rel sits up in his tree. On-ly one small nut has he.

Let us go, you and me, with a sack-ful for his tea.

MI

RE

DO

# DREAMING

*SO    MI    RE DO*

We were fly - ing, Ted - dy and I.
Moon and stars were pas-sing us by.

We saw such a love-ly rain-bow. "It's so pret-ty," Ted-dy said.

"But I think we must be dream-ing 'cos you see we're still in bed."

SO
MI
RE
DO

## SUSIE SNAIL

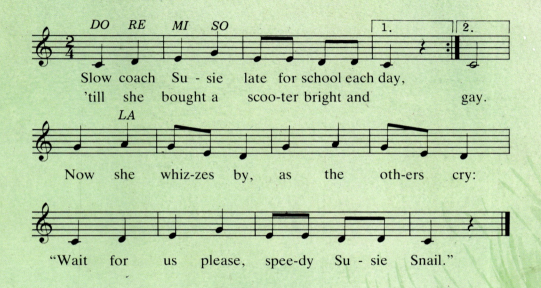

DO RE MI SO

1.   2.

Slow coach Su - sie late for school each day,
'till she bought a scoo-ter bright and gay.

LA

Now she whiz-zes by, as the oth-ers cry:

"Wait for us please, spee-dy Su - sie Snail."

R

S

T

U

LA
SO
MI
RE
DO

# LONELY FROG

On my stone, all a- lone, someone's friend I want to be.

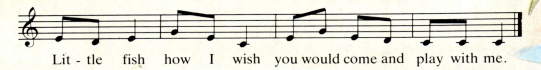

Lit - tle fish how I wish you would come and play with me.

14

LA
SO
MI
RE
DO

# LITTLE GNAT

SO  LA  DO

1. Lit - tle gnat sat on a wall feel-ing ve - ry jol - ly,

'till he had a lit - tle fall, now he's mel - an - cho - ly.

2. Doctor sent him straight to bed
   with his cuts and scratches.
   Then got from the First Aid Kit
   bandages and patches.

3. Everybody visited,
   bringing fruit and jelly,
   sitting on his feather bed
   watching films on telly.

4. Little gnat sat on the wall
   feeling very jolly.
   Now he's careful not to fall
   he's not melancholy.

5. After that the little gnat
   thought his life was boring
   on his little feather sat,
   said: "let's go exploring."

6. Feather floated high and free
   'till he heard gnat grumble:
   "If the world is round then we
   off the end will tumble."

7. On they floated hand in hand,
   over seas uncharted,
   'till at last they came to land,
   right back where they started.

8. Little gnat sat on the ground
   said: "My life's not boring,
   now I know the world is round
   and I've been exploring."

16

# WONKY DONKEY

LA  RE  DO  MI

Don-key's won-ky dear-ie me. Oh don-key! What a won-ky

don-key he, oh don-key! Won-ky don-key come with us.

Oh don-key! Hur-ry or we'll miss the bus. Oh don-key!

2. What a stubborn mule you are, oh donkey!
Come on Wonky it's not far. Oh donkey!
Making such a dreadful fuss. Oh donkey!
Now you've made us miss the bus. Oh donkey!

18

MI
RE
DO
LA

# SPRINGTIME

MI LA    DO    RE LA      SO

Bare-foot on the grass I'm sit - ting, Butt - er - flies a-

round me flit - ting. Danc-ing, sing-ing, I'm so cle-

ver. I wish spring would last for ev - er.

LA

SO

MI

RE

DO

LA

**LA**

**DO**

**RE**

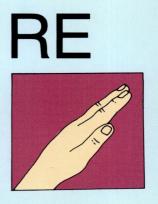

**MI**

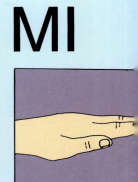

**SO**

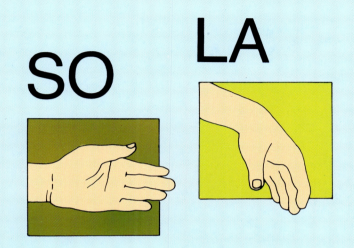

**LA**

**DO**

## MESSAGE FROM DR. GÉZA SZILVAY
### Head of the East Helsinki Music Institute and compiler of the
### "Singing Rascals" series

Many children today have all the material things they need: clothes, food, toys, etc; sometimes they have more than enough. Material things, however, cannot replace the warmth affection and time we give to the child, which is so important for its spiritual nourishment.

The "Singing Rascals" books are intended as a means of helping parents, grandparents, kindergarten and nursery school teachers, and all those who have children in their care, to create stimulating and purposeful moments with them.

The pictures, melodies, and words in these books have been carefully chosen and arranged with young pre-school children in mind. The tunes have been selected from those which over the years have proved appealing and easy to learn, and are skilfully illustrated. The characters may be used to make up tales arising from the songs. The printed notation is only for the use of the adults.

The songs progress from two notes up to five notes (pentatonic) or seven notes (diatonic). Although for the sake of clarity they are written in C major and A minor, singing them in different keys, i.e. from different starting notes, is to be encouraged, thus suiting the children's own pitch registers. The use of solfa marking (Do-Re) makes it easy for parents to learn basic solmisation while the children enjoy learning the pitch names and hand signs.

The series is supported by a parallel series of audio tapes on which infants sing and young children perform the melodies, but no cassette, however good, can replace the lap and guidance of the close relative or friend.

The creation of Colourstrings Music Kindergartens is a significant step forward in the music education of the very young, and one in which I feel proud to play a part. My wish for all the little members is – joyous singing!

Géza Szilvay

Composers:

**Look Lamb Look**
*

**Harry Hare**
*

**Hey Beetle!**
*

**Squirrel**
Jorma Ollaranta

**Dreaming**
Zoltán Kodály
© 1962 by Zoltán Kodály
Copyright assigned 1964 to
Boosey & Hawkes Music Publishers Ltd
Revised Edition © 1970 by
Boosey & Hawkes Music Publishers Ltd
Reprinted by permission of
Boosey & Hawkes Music Publishers Ltd

**Susie Snail**
Pál Járdányi
© 1973 by Editio Musica Budapest

**Lonely Frog**
Zoltán Kodály
© 1962 by Zoltán Kodály
Copyright assigned 1964 to
Boosey & Hawkes Music Publishers Ltd
Revised Edition © 1970 by
Boosey & Hawkes Music Publishers Ltd
Reprinted by permission of
Boosey & Hawkes Music Publishers Ltd

**Little Gnat**
Zoltán Kodály
© 1962 by Zoltán Kodály
Copyright assigned 1964 to
Boosey & Hawkes Music Publishers Ltd
Revised Edition © 1970 by
Boosey & Hawkes Music Publishers Ltd
Reprinted by permission of
Boosey & Hawkes Music Publishers Ltd

**Wonky Donkey**
Zoltán Kodály
© 1941 by Zoltán Kodály
Copyright assigned 1963 to
Boosey & Company Ltd
Revised Edition © 1972 by
Boosey & Company Ltd
Reprinted by permission of
Boosey & Hawkes Music Publishers Ltd

**Springtime**
*

*Tunes based on children's and folk melodies.